I0158169

What's Up With That?

Humorous Short Stories About Life in Modern-Day America

Gloria Hander Lyons

Blue Sage Press

What's Up With That?
Humorous Short Stories About
Life in Modern-Day America

Copyright © 2009 by Gloria Hander Lyons

All Rights Reserved. No part of this book may be reproduced or utilized in any form or by any means, electronic or mechanical, including but not limited to photocopying, recording, or by any information storage and retrieval system without the prior written permission of the author.

Inquires should be addressed to:
Blue Sage Press
48 Borondo Pines
La Marque, TX 77568
www.BlueSagePress.com

ISBN: 978-0-9842438-0-8

Library of Congress Control Number: 2009937543

First Edition: October 2009

The information in this book is true and complete to the best of our knowledge. All recommendations are made without guarantee on the part of the author or Blue Sage Press. The author and publisher disclaim any liability in connection with the use of this information.

Printed in the United States of America

Table of Contents

What's Up With That?

Introduction

Have you ever encountered a situation that seemed so bizarre your only response was, "What's up with that?"

This book includes 19 humorous short stories that depict a few of these "head-scratching" moments you might have encountered at some point during your life.

If you've ever eaten at a restaurant where the lights were so dim you couldn't see your food, been trapped in an elevator with someone wearing so much cologne you couldn't breathe, or been stuck in a traffic jam in the "drive-thru" lane at a fast food restaurant, then you can relate!

Life in modern-day America can be challenging—to say the least—so why not look at the humorous side and vent some of our stress through chuckling instead of exploding?

Most Americans can empathize with the experiences I've written about in this volume. So take a few moments to sit down, relax and enjoy these light-hearted tales.

I encounter topics for my "what's up with that?" stories frequently as I go about the chores of my daily life and plan to write about many more of them.

I love to receive feedback from my readers and would especially like to hear your "what's up with that?" tales.

If you'd like to share your own frustrating dilemmas from everyday life, e-mail your comments to:

gloria@bluesagepress.com

Or send them in writing to:

Gloria Lyons
Blue Sage Press
48 Borondo Pines
La Marque, TX 77568

Just remember to keep it light and keep it tactful, because life is semi-humorous.

The Point of
No Return

If I had to bet money when I gambled on picking the fastest-moving line at the grocery store check-out counter, I'd be stone-cold broke. Even after putting all my observation powers into play—examining the skills of the check-out clerk, tallying up the number of items in each cart in front of me, and noting the preferred payment of each customer—it never fails, I always wind up in the line that drags along slower than molasses in January. What's up with that?

This scenario is further compounded by the fact that I shop at super discount stores; those one-stop-shopping mega-stores that sell everything from soup to furniture. There I stand, inching my overloaded shopping cart along, watching my ice cream melt and ooze down the side of the already sticky container.

And just when I'm lured into a false sense of optimism that I might escape before hell freezes over while my ice cream melts, the dreaded check-out light begins to blink, signaling the manager that there's a problem on the line— a question about price, a method of payment or a missing item.

As I inch closer to the conveyor belt, I'm forced to make the final commitment to this register. Do I dare remove my items from the cart? I'll be forfeiting a chance to make the break for a shorter, faster-moving line.

After a nail-biting moment, I begin to unload my cart. Then the customer in front of me wails, "What do you mean these shoes are $6.98? The sign said $5.98!"

On goes the blinking light, while the clerk makes a futile call to the shoe department for confirmation.

We all know there's no one in the shoe department. Even if, on the outside chance, someone did answer the phone, there's no way to check the price on a pair of mismatched shoes in the wrong box that are left over from last season's inventory. But it doesn't matter; the light keeps on blinking while we all keep on waiting...and waiting.

While debating whether to pile the items back into my cart or offer to give the woman a dollar to cover the difference in price, the clerk gets the totally unexpected call from the shoe department. It's a miracle! They've confirmed the woman's claim and we're on the move again—briefly.

"Do you have a pen?" the woman asks the clerk.

Shouldn't there be a law that says anyone carrying a checkbook must also be required to carry a pen? This woman had been standing in line for at least fifteen minutes and hadn't made the slightest plan for making payment.

My knuckles turned white as I gripped the shopping cart handle. Finally, it was my turn to check out. My ice cream sloshed around inside the carton as it rolled down the conveyor belt.

Would I never learn? What's the point of saving a few cents on a carton of ice cream at a discount superstore when it can't survive the trip to the car?

I sighed and stepped up to the cash register for my long-awaited turn; my credit card at the ready. I certainly wasn't going to hold up the line with arguments over price or fumbling around looking for my card. I was a considerate shopper!

The clerk gave me a perky smile; then turned off her cash register light. "Sorry, ma'am, this lane is closed."

Pondering the Here-After

More and more frequently, I find myself standing in the middle of a room thinking about the "here after".

No, I'm not talking about life after death and seeing bright, white lights. I'm talking about: "The lights are on but nobody's home." I can't remember what I came in here after.

I left the kitchen to get something in the bedroom, but somewhere during my fifteen-second commute, my brain jumped to the next page and now its "back button" is no longer functioning. What's up with that?

I guess I can chalk it up to "older" age, but since my brain circuit mishaps are becoming more of a problem, I actually did some research on this phenomenon. The experts say it happens because we're trying to do too many things at once.

We're not "living in the moment". Instead, we're already thinking about what we need to do next before we've finished our current task. They tell us we need to focus on the present instead of operating on auto-pilot with a million other thoughts zinging around in our brains.

Then we wouldn't forget where we put our car keys, or whether we locked the back door when we left the house, or forget to change our house slippers for shoes before we leave.

This seems like perfectly sound advice. I'd love to live in the moment—if I was a jet-setting millionaire or a glamorous movie star. But let's get real! My lifestyle moments involve stacks of food-encrusted dishes and mountains of dirty laundry. No wonder I'm always thinking about the here-after—or anywhere but here!

I have to admit, though, sometimes it pays to focus on the task at hand. I have a tendency to operate on auto pilot more often than not, which can be downright scary—especially when I arrive at the shopping mall and can't remember driving through the traffic light at the intersection of Main and Highway 3. With that kind of focus, I might be seeing that bright, white light sooner than later.

But the really annoying thing about not focusing on the present is that I'm now standing in the mall parking lot and I don't have a clue where I parked my car. It's strange; I don't even remember driving myself here.

Wait. I didn't drive here. I came with my husband. Hallelujah! I knew I'd figure it out. The experts are right; if you try to stay focused, everything will work out fine.

Now I just need to focus on where I saw my husband last. Was it the food court or the sporting goods store?

Here's an ugly thought; maybe he had a "here-after" moment and left without me!

Hanging Around

While sitting in my car at a traffic light recently, I noticed a passing vehicle with a collection of shiny Mardi Gras beads dangling from the rear view mirror. This vehicle was followed by another whose mirror sported a colorful Hawaiian lei.

My curiosity piqued, I began to survey other cars in the vicinity for signs of "auto décor" and much to my surprise, most were trimmed like Christmas trees with an array of unusual items. What's up with that?

I stared at my own unadorned mirror, which suddenly seemed sadly neglected. Was I asleep at the wheel when this new trend swept into vogue? I'm an interior decorator, for goodness sake, but somehow decorating the interior spaces of my car had never occurred to me.

I've never hung anything from my car's rear view mirror, although I must confess, I have, in the distant past, contributed to mirror décor. Many, many years ago, when I was in high school, I taught myself to knit; my project was a pair of baby booties.

When my cousin managed to snag a brand new 1966 pale yellow Chevy Super Sport with black interior, I made him a pair of color-coordinated baby booties to hang from his rear-view mirror. I thought they were super cool. I was fifteen; I didn't know any better. He was eighteen; he should have!

Perhaps I needed to research this new auto décor trend. Considering the amount of time we spend in our vehicles commuting each day and sitting at a stand-still in bumper-to-bumper traffic, it actually makes sense to enhance our captive environments.

I began to take note of the variety of objects that drivers pressed into service to flaunt their personal decorating style.

Many owners hung religious artifacts, such as rosaries or crosses from their mirrors. Not a bad idea given the fact that you're taking your life into your hands while traveling on today's highways. We can use all the help we can get.

The Mardi Gras beads are quite eye-catching. It's always a good plan to decorate your space with items that represent fond memories—as long as those memories don't include the remnants of a hangover from too much "partying" the night before. Then you and the other drivers on the road might be better served with a religious icon.

I also noticed an alarming number of air fresheners (in the shape of little trees). That can't possibly be a good sign. What objectionable smells are these drivers trying to hide? Too many fast-food meals eaten in haste while in transit; the food wrappers jammed carelessly underneath their car seats? Or last week's sweaty work-out clothes from the gym? It's a heavy price to pay.

My most bizarre sighting, however, occurred in the parking lot at the grocery store. The car parked nose-to-nose with mine had a stuffed frog playing a tiny guitar hanging from the rear view mirror. He sported an Elvis wig and satin cape. I was mesmerized. No way was I going to leave that lot without getting a glimpse of the driver. So I waited, while my ice cream melted.

Soon, an elderly, gray-haired woman appeared beside the car. Large earrings, made from dominoes, dangled from her earlobes. They featured a hand-painted image of Elvis' face.

She wore a long, silky caftan—also hand-painted with scenes of her favorite rock and roll star. As she hoisted her hefty handbag onto the front seat, the sun glinted off the rhinestone-studded "E" emblazoned on the front.

I watched as she back out of the parking space and sped off toward what I'm certain was her own personal version of "Graceland", her domino earrings swinging to the beat of "Jail House Rock" blaring on the CD player.

Once again, I stared at my unadorned rear view mirror and vowed, "It's time to decorate!"

The Battle at the Pump

I never thought I'd see the day when gasoline would be worth its weight in gold! These days, if you own a large vehicle, you need to take out a bank loan to fill the tank. And the price of gasoline just keeps going up. It fluctuates, not monthly or weekly, but sometimes hourly! The same gas that was sitting in the pump an hour ago is suddenly valued at ten cents per gallon more. What's up with that?

Yesterday morning, I drove into my favorite gas station (the one that usually has the lowest price in town) to fill the tank before heading off to run a few errands. I removed the gas cap and began pumping the "liquid gold", watching in horror as the dollar amount whirled by at an alarming rate.

It was too depressing to watch, so I distracted myself with the surrounding scenery until the pump clicked off, hoping my credit card wouldn't go into melt-down when I paid the final bill.

As I scanned the activity at the other pumps, Darren, the station owner, left his office, carrying a large plastic sign. He glanced around furtively, then skulked across the lot, heading for the price display out front.

A chill ran down my spine when I realized he planned to change the gasoline price. So far, I'd pumped six gallons; my tank needed at least another six.

I squeezed the nozzle trigger harder, hoping to increase the flow, but the numbers seemed to crawl by at an agonizingly slow pace.

Seven gallons down, five to go, as Darren placed a step ladder under the price sign and began his evil deed of raising the already outrageous price. To what? I couldn't see the number printed on the sign he carried.

"Hurry!" I screeched at the gasoline nozzle, shaking it in a futile attempt to fill my tank faster.

This couldn't be legal. Was he allowed to change the price of gas in mid-fill? Did he have a magic button that he pushed to raise the price at all the pumps before his customers finished filling their tanks? Where's the justice?

Darren stepped onto the bottom rung of the ladder, holding the large sign at his side. I could see the number on it now. It was a three. Was he planning to raise the price from $2.89 per gallon to three dollars per gallon? Unbelievable!

I kicked the pump and banged on the side. "Faster!" I yelled, startling the customers nearby. Ten gallons down, only two more to go.

Slowly, Darren began to climb the ladder—closer and closer to the top, dragging the dreaded sign behind him. I glanced at the pump read-out; eleven gallons. I danced around in desperation as he reached the top step. Was I going to lose this battle after all?

But just when I was ready to throw in the towel, the pump clicked off. "Yes!" I cried, as Darren reached up to change the sign.

I hung up the nozzle quicker than a gunslinger in a Western movie, then raised both hands above my head in the "international sign of victory", turning to face the cheering crowds (or, in this case, gawking onlookers).

But my moment of triumph was quickly replaced by the agony of defeat, as I watched Darren place the number "3" on the price display sign—not over the "2" in $2.89, but over the "9". Once again, I kicked the pump in frustration.

"Touché," I sighed, saluting Darren on his victory, as I drove off into the brilliant orange sunrise.

Still smarting, however, from the sting of defeat, I narrowed my eyes in a defiant glare. "Until we meet again—next week!"

Just One
Little Candle

My friend, Donna, and I decided to treat ourselves to lunch the other day at one of those upscale, downtown, trendy restaurants. Anticipation was high, as we donned our best outfits and headed for the big city.

When we arrived, however, our expectations were doused—or I should say dimmed. The restaurant interior was so dark, we barely avoided bumping into the furniture and other diners on the way to our table. What's up with that?

Andrew, our waiter, handed us each a menu, which of course we couldn't read for lack of illumination. Instead, we simply chose to listen to the specials for the day.

"I'll have that," Donna said, when Andrew paused for a breath.

"Me, too," I added.

While waiting for our food to arrive, we squinted into the darkness, hoping to catch a glimpse of the supposedly elegant décor—not a chance. We might as well have been dining in Carlsbad Caverns, with the lights out.

"Do you think there are bats up there?" asked Donna, scanning the shadowy depths above us.

While we pondered the spooky prospect of bats hanging over our heads, Andrew brought a basket of freshly baked rolls to our table. We knew this because our mouths began to water with the heavenly aroma. Locating the basket, however, was another matter.

"Ouch," said Donna. "That's my arm!"

"Sorry," I replied, "I was reaching for a roll."

Next, Andrew brought our entrees, placing them deftly in front of us. We squinted, trying to make out the objects on our plates.

"Could we have a bit more light?" asked Donna.

With a flourish, Andrew whipped a fancy, long-handled lighter from his apron and lit the tiny votive candle in the center of the table.

"We're going to need about five or six more of those," I said.

Andrew gave me a haughty glare, then turned to leave. He kissed his tip good bye!

"What do you think this is?" asked Donna, stabbing a piece of food and holding it up for my inspection.

I pulled out my trusty penlight attached to my key ring and directed a tiny beam of light at her fork. "A shrimp," I declared.

"Yum!" she replied.

We continued to stab blindly at our food until we began to feel full. Now I know how Helen Keller must have felt. I just love that movie.

I rubbed my fingers around on my plate to make sure I hadn't overlooked something. Nope—all gone. I licked the tasty sauce from my fingers and waved my napkin in the air, hoping to attract Andrew's attention.

"Check, Madame?" he asked, suddenly appearing from the darkness.

"Please," I replied.

Now, I'm not saying I won't go back to that restaurant. The food was quite good. But I have one request for all you restaurant owners out there. Could you lighten things up a bit? Being able to see your food, as well as taste and smell it would add a whole new dimension to the dining experience.

Imagine that! Well, actually, I wouldn't have to, if I could see it!

Stuck
on You

Our lives these days are pushed along at break-neck speed, mainly because of all the high-tech, computerized devices we encounter at every turn. Bar codes are a good example of how technology has sped up the check out process at most retail stores.

Each item has one of those little paper bar code tags glued to it, so the checkout clerk can scan your items in record time. That's the good news. The bad news is that you need a degree in chemical engineering to remove those little tags from your newly acquired possessions. What's up with that?

A few days ago, I accidentally broke my ceramic salt shaker—the one with the pretty blue flowers on it that matches my dinnerware. Yes, I know—bad luck. I dumped the broken pieces in the trash, tossed a handful of salt over my left shoulder for good measure, and called an 800 number to order a replacement.

I was delighted when the new shaker arrived; unfortunately, it had one of those bar code stickers stuck to the side. Just the sight of it sent chills down my spine! Everyone knows those things are impossible to remove.

I tugged at the corner gently, trying not to tear the paper; but lost that battle, as the top layer separated, leaving me with a thin layer of paper over a thick layer of glue. I clawed desperately at the sticky residue with my fingernails, but only managed to reshape it into a brown glob.

Moving along to the chemical phase, I washed the shaker inside and out with detergent; but the gummy glob remained. Next, I tried window cleaner; perhaps the ammonia would do the trick. Nope—no luck. Scouring powder, I thought. Surely that will work. Not a chance. I now had grimy little particles mixed in with the sticky glue.

In a last-ditch effort, I dashed out to the work shop in search of sand paper. I wasn't fooling around anymore! But that turned out to be a mistake; now I had big gritty particles in addition to little gritty particles mixed in with the steadfast glue.

I gave up, washed and filled the shaker with salt, and put it on the dinner table. I figured in maybe five or ten years, after a few more washings, it was bound to come off.

At dinner that night, my husband asked, "Hon, would you pass me the salt?"

"Sure," I replied, handing him the brand new shaker.

"You need to let go," he said, trying to remove it from my hand.

"I can't, it's stuck."

"What do you mean, it's stuck?"

"It's the glue from the bar code label," I explained.

"You mean you didn't even wash it?" he was dumb enough to ask.

I glared at him. I should have thrown the stupid shaker at him. And I would have, too, if it wasn't permanently attached to my hand.

A Heavy Load

Have you noticed, as you get older, your metabolic rate keeps getting slower; and even though you're eating the same amount of food, you just keep gaining weight? What's up with that? Life just isn't fair!

Not only is your body burning fewer calories, it just can't seem to function at the same physical level it once did. In my mid-thirties, I bounced through an hour of high-impact aerobics four times a week; and then went home to enjoy a bowl of my favorite ice cream. I weighed 105 pounds!

Now, however, my knees can no longer handle the pounding of an aerobics workout. I struggle through thirty minutes on an elliptical trainer five days a week, I haven't tasted real ice cream in fifteen years, and don't even *think* about asking me how much I weigh!

A brisk thirty-minute walk three times a week, as suggested by today's health care professionals, won't use up enough calories to burn off even *half* a Big Mac. At that rate, I figure, in five years, I'll have a Big Mac stuck to each hip, one on each bun, and one covering my belly button!

Believe me, this is one sick joke that Mother Nature is perpetrating on the "not-so-young-anymore." We've paid our dues, worked hard all our lives, and just when we reach the age where we can afford to relax and enjoy the fruits of our labor, fruit is about all we're going to get unless we want to be as big as a house!

I finally realized that I have no choice but to cut back on calories. Last night, as I served dinner to my husband, he stared at his plate, frowning.

"Hon, is there a problem with the budget?" he asked, poking his finger at the five Cheerios artfully arranged around a baby carrot.

"No," I replied. "We're cutting back."

"On what? Life? I figure, with these portions, I've got maybe thirty days left before I starve—forty tops, if I get seconds!"

I glared at him, jumped up from the table, rummaged through the fridge and plopped, not one, but *two* baby carrots on his plate.

"There," I said. "Are you happy now?"

I knew in my heart, however, that a fast-food visit was looming large in his future—about twenty minutes was my best outside guess. And, yes, I'd probably be there, right beside him.

Have you tried those baked apple pies? Yum!

The Evil
Fast-Food
Drive-Thru
Hoax

I've decided to blow the whistle on the evil "drive-thru hoax" that American fast food restaurants have perpetrated on their unsuspecting (or unwitting) customers. While sitting in one of my favorite fast food restaurants the other day (yes, I'm a fast food junkie), I counted eight cars parked in the drive thru lane. Eight! What's up with that?

Do these gullible souls actually think they're going to get faster service in the drive thru lane? NOT!!! Even if it takes only five minutes per customer—if you're lucky—to take an order, receive payment and hand over the bag, guy number eight is looking at a good thirty-five-minute wait.

With the high price of gasoline these days, who can afford to sit with the engine running for that length of time; all for the sake of cheap food and "fast" (I use that term lightly) service?

Considering the number of calories we scarf down with our "super-sized" meals, parking and hiking into the restaurant would burn off at least a few calories. Heck, we'd all be better off parking at the fast food joint at the end of the block and jogging back to this one. Then we could eat those fries *almost* guilt free.

But, there they sit in the "drive-thru" lane—inching along and waiting, while sucking up the toxic fumes from the car in front of them. Maybe that's the problem: brain damage from car fumes in drive thru lanes. I can see it now, a whole new class of law suits!

As I enjoyed my meal in air-conditioned comfort, the long line of cars continued to snake through the lane outside. Occasionally, one pulled off to the side to wait even longer for his "special" order to be delivered.

And then there was the poor sucker, directed to the sidelines, and his order was lost in the process. Ten minutes later, he stomped inside to complain.

But the real kicker is the guy who gets back to his office and discovers that he received the wrong order. Now that's entertainment!

Ah, such is life in the drive thru lane. It's enough to make you want to brown-bag your own lunch—or not. As for me, I'll gladly park my car and walk inside, whether I'm getting my food to go or eating it on site. I'm certainly not going to burn up a gallon of gasoline and inhale toxic fumes in the hope of saving myself a few steps.

Like I said before, there's no such thing as "drive thru" at a fast food restaurant. If these places were forced to adhere to truth in advertising, the sign would actually read, "Park and Wait Lane".

But don't mind me. This is a free country. If you want to waste your time and gas, kill off your brain cells and hoard your calories, be my guest.

Oh, and for those of you who are feeling a bit dizzy, call 1-800-LAWYERS.

Is It Hot
in Here?

Have you ever experienced the dreaded malaise that afflicts women on the downside of forty, where your skin turns a bright shade of red and feels like it's on fire? Then your own personal sprinkler system goes off, drenching you from head to toe, soaking your clothing with perspiration.

Jokingly referred to by the uninitiated as a "hot flash", it's a cruel trick Mother Nature plays on females past their prime. What's up with that?

Weren't we tortured enough during child-birth, followed by years of juggling motherhood and housework—many times including the added stress of a career? Then, just when we breathe a sigh of relief that we actually survived the mayhem, and rejoice over the extra space of an "empty nest", we're hit with a whole new dilemma: uncomfortable, dehydrating, embarrassing, sleep-depriving hot flashes. What's a mature woman to do?

After a month of being awakened twelve times every night, usually involving one or more changes of my sweat-soaked nightgown and bed sheets, I ran screaming to my gynecologist's office, demanding relief.

"I can prescribe hormone-replacement therapy," she offered, reluctantly, "but there can be health risks involved."

I stared at her in disbelief. "What about the health risks from sleep deprivation?" I argued. "Like insanity, for instance, or falling asleep at the wheel while driving, or murdering someone in a fit of rage!"

After observing my wild-eyed expression, my flushed complexion, the perspiration trickling down the side of my face, and the bald spots on my scalp where I'd torn out patches of hair in frustration, she made the calculated decision to hand over the drugs.

"Here's a one-year prescription and a sample pack," she said, as I lunged for the small, blue packet that she held tight in her grasp.

I swallowed one of the pills before leaving the office, hoping for instant relief, but was devastated to learn that it could take days, maybe weeks, before the torturous flashes would begin to subside.

That night, after getting ready for bed, my husband, Bob, came into the bedroom and found me lying on top of the down comforter, wearing my skimpiest summer nightie (in the dead of winter), with the ceiling fan going full-blast. "Hon?" he asked, with a gleam in his eye. "Are you feeling frisky tonight?"

"Don't touch me!" I screeched, frantically fanning my red hot cheeks.

Startled, he retreated to a safer distance. "Didn't you take your pill?"

I glared at him, as the perspiration pooling in my belly button overflowed and trickled down my side.

"Maybe you should take another one," he suggested.

My eyes widened with hope, but a few mathematical calculations dashed the possibility. My doctor gave me a one year prescription, renewable only at my next office visit. If I doubled up on the pills, I'd run out in six months. And that could be disastrous!

Bob hesitated, weighing his options, while eyeing my futile fanning, twitching and flailing. "How long does one of these flashes last?"

"Forty-eight seconds," I replied, with precision accuracy.

"Oh," he said. "That's not too bad."

"Then I'll have another one thirty minutes later. And then another one, and another one..." My wild-eyed expression had returned.

With a hint of panic in his voice, Bob reassessed the situation. "Maybe I'll just sleep on the couch tonight."

I have to hand it to him. The man is a quick study.

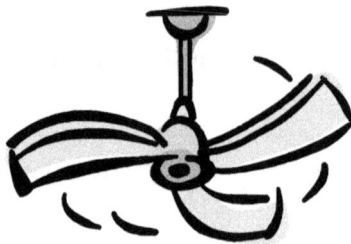

Do You Feel Lucky?

I'm a writer by trade; therefore, it stands to reason that I'm also an avid reader. I read everything: books, magazines, newspapers, labels—even those tiny tags attached to pillows that say, "Do not remove under penalty of death".

I'm also a firm believer in reading directions: cooking directions, map directions, and especially the directions from manufacturers for assembling furniture, toys and other paraphernalia.

It seems, however, that the general population falls into two categories when it comes to reading instruction manuals: those who read directions and those who don't. My husband and son fall into the second category; they simply refuse to read assembly instructions. What's up with that?

They way I see it—even if the directions are vague or confusing, I'm still better off reading them than starting the assembly process without a clue. But the men in my family disagree.

"Don't you want to read the instructions first?" I ask.

"Nah," they reply, "We can figure it out."

I'm not sure whether these "pro" or "anti" instruction-reading groups are aligned by gender or personality traits, but I'm firmly planted in the "pro" group.

When I'm faced with an assembly project, I count and identify all the parts, just like the manual suggests. I read through the entire list of steps to make sure I understand the process. Then I begin the task. My time is valuable, and I don't want to discover several hours in to the process that I'm missing a part or that I've installed the door upside down. My husband, Bob, calls this behavior "compulsive", but I'm not convinced that his method is more effective.

On a recent spring day, Bob and I made one of our frequent visits to the local home improvement store. We stopped dead in our tracks just inside the entrance. There in front of us was a colorful backyard display featuring a double-size outdoor swing on a free-standing frame with comfy cushions and a canopy overhead.

"Wow," Bob said. "That would be great in the backyard."

I had to agree. I pictured myself lounging on those cushions underneath the canopy's shade with a great book and a tall glass of ice tea.

"Let's buy it," Bob said.

I surveyed the boxes stacked beside the swing. How did they get that monstrous contraption inside such a tiny box? "Maybe we should buy the assembly service, too," I said.

"No way, there's nothing to it," he replied.

We loaded up the box and whisked it away to our backyard. Bob tore open the package and dumped out a gazillion parts and a twenty-page manual.

"Do you want me to read the instructions while you assemble each step?" I asked futilely.

"Nah," came the reply I expected. "Just go inside and I'll call you when it's ready. This shouldn't take more than an hour."

Two hours later, I wandered outside to check on the progress. The sun was dipping low in the sky. "How's it going?" I asked.

"I think I've just about figured it out," he mumbled, wiping the sweat and grease from his forehead.

I sighed, glancing at the instruction manual tossed carelessly onto the back porch. To his credit, however, he had made some progress. The frame was assembled, and there were now only half a gazillion parts scattered around the yard.

"Are you sure you don't want me to read the directions for you?" I asked once again.

"I'm fine. I'll have this together in no time. You'll see."

Two hours later, he popped inside the backdoor. "It's ready," he grinned. "Come and see."

By now the sun had set and total darkness enveloped the backyard. I turned on the porch light, grabbed a flashlight and scurried off to see our new outdoor oasis.

On the way through the yard, I stumbled over an object on the ground. I aimed my flashlight at what appeared to be a long, angled piece of metal.

"What's this?" I asked.

"They always give you extra parts," Bob replied.

I hefted the bar and turned it over in my hand. "This is a pretty substantial piece of metal," I said. "They gave us two of these?"

"I didn't need it," he explained. "They just throw in all those extra braces for overkill."

My eyebrows shot up to the top of my head while I waited for more details.

"This swing is perfectly stable without that part," he argued. "Try it out."

I examined the metal support in my hand, noticing the two holes in each end intended for heavy bolts. I did a quick mental tally of Bob's life insurance coverage and smiled, "You first."

Burning the Midnight Oil

Sleep is not only important for our health and well-being, it's critical for preserving our sanity. With the hectic pace and stressful work conditions most people endure in today's society, it's a miracle we get any sleep at all.

For the most part, I manage to squeeze in the minimum number of hours recommended by modern health care professionals, but it seems that my most creative, thought-provoking, life-changing ideas arrive at two in the morning. What's up with that?

These sudden flashes of super-charged brain activity occur during the twilight hours when my mind is free-floating between sleep and consciousness; totally unrestrained by rational thinking.

My early morning brainstorming sessions don't involve earth-shattering issues, but they wreak havoc on restful sleep: what title should I use for an exciting new book idea, what tasty treats can I concoct to dazzle my Bunco club members, how can I get rid of the piano in the dining room without my husband noticing that it's gone?

Once my brain latches on to one of these high-octane ideas, it races non-stop at full throttle. Sleep is not an option. Sometimes these events last for hours; completely out of my control.

I immediately shift into mental attack mode, intent on solving the problem at hand, but by morning I've forgotten every detail. The only remnant of this predawn anguish is "brain fog" from lack of sleep.

Other times, I remember the entire process but discover that what seemed like a brilliant idea at two am is ridiculous drivel when examined by the light of the following sleep-deprived day.

In desperation, I placed a flashlight, pen and pad of paper by my bed. As soon as one of my brain storms began, I could record the flash of brilliance, hoping to postpone another non-stop planning session during the wee hours of the morning.

It worked. I was able to get back to sleep in less than an hour. The next day, however, when I scanned my notes, I realized I was writing so fast, in a futile attempt to keep pace with my thoughts, my words were totally indecipherable.

My conclusion: I needed a tape recorder. Unfortunately, this solution involved leaving the bedroom to avoid disturbing my husband during the night, but I was determined to resolve my sleep-interruption issues.

I took the plunge and purchased one of those micro-mini recorders. It's about the size of a potato chip, so it doesn't take up much space, but it's also easy to lose. This ever-diminishing size for electronic gadgets seems to be a common theme for advancing technology, but that's another story I'll save for a later date.

The next time my brain went into overdrive, I stumbled out of bed and into the kitchen. Three kitchen drawers later, I found the elusive recorder, but couldn't read the tiny buttons on that modern-day miracle.

I searched frantically for my reading glasses, but even those didn't help my plight. I still couldn't figure out how to make the darn machine record. I pushed, pulled, rattled and banged that wretched piece of technology to no avail, then finally tossed it in the trash and stomped back to the bedroom.

The muffled laughter from my husband's side of the bed did nothing to improve my mood. "Trying to save the world again?" he chuckled.

I kicked off my house shoes and jerked the bed covers over my head. "Just the living room," I groaned. "Do you think if we moved the television into the corner and brought the two chairs in from the family room..." By then my husband was snoring again.

It was going to be another long and sleepless night.

A Little Dab'll Do Ya

Have you ever been stuck in the close confines of an elevator with a person (man or woman) who's wearing so much cologne you found it difficult to breathe without gagging? You can't help but wonder if they've totally lost their sense of smell, or if their friends or loved ones simply don't have the heart to speak up. What's up with that?

I know the perfume industry is partly to blame for this anti-social faux pas. The "dab-on" perfume bottles are no longer available in most scents, so you're forced to buy spray bottles. And we all know what's up with that! The industry wants everyone to use five times more cologne than they need, so they run out five times faster and buy five times more. That's good news for the perfume business, but bad news for those of us unfortunate enough to be in close proximity to these overly-scented bodies.

So, what's the answer to this dilemma? Toss out those spray pumps and spread the word. Where cologne is concerned, "a little dab'll do ya".

In some cases, using too much cologne can be costly business-wise, as well as social-wise, if you can't sneak up on someone because your scent arrives long before you do.

A television commercial that aired quite a few years ago demonstrated this point perfectly. It showed a group of office workers playing on the job; then one employee sniffed the air and sounded the alarm. "He's coming!" A few seconds later, the highly-scented, unsuspecting boss arrived to find all his employees hard at work. Sometimes the element of surprise can be very useful.

Have you ever treated yourself and your partner to a special dinner at a nice restaurant only to have your "Trout Amandine" turned into "Trout de Par fume" by an overzealous perfume user seated nearby? Knowing how our sense of smell affects our taste buds, I'm surprised restaurant owners don't post bouncers at the door to snag these "odorous offenders", following the lead of bar owners for handling their offensive customers.

How do you know if you've applied too much? If the smell of your cologne arrives quite a while before you do; if anyone, other than a bloodhound, can follow your cologne-scented trail; or if you're surrounded by a potent, perfumed cloud, leaving others coughing in your wake, you probably qualify.

It would behoove all scent users to perform the "hide and sniff" test before leaving home. After applying (hopefully not spraying) your cologne, hide. Then see if your partner can find you by following your scent. If you can't decide whether or not your cologne is too strong for public exposure, please enlist the aid of a second, honest opinion.

As for the rest of us poor, tortured souls who get trapped in close confinement with a cologne abuser, how long can you hold your breath?

Breathing
Room

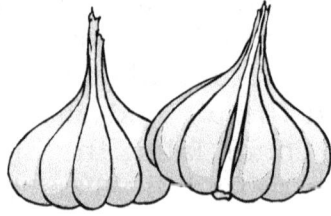

Did I miss something? Did my brain zone out for the last several years during a social revolution that made garlic the "king" of food flavors? How did garlic become a socially acceptable breath scent? During the era when I was growing up, garlic breath was a social taboo. Now it's virtually impossible to avoid. What's up with that?

As part of a recent quest to eat healthier, I tried one of those "lean" frozen microwave meals for lunch. Unfortunately, the garlic flavor was so overpowering I felt like a garlic-breathing dragon for the rest of the day. These days, no matter what restaurant cuisine you choose—Mexican, French, Chinese or Italian—every single dish is loaded with garlic. Even a good old American comfort food, like mashed potatoes, has morphed into the trendy "garlic" mashed potatoes. And the offensive odor lingers on your breath for hours; sometimes days.

No one wants to expose their fellow co-workers to "post-lunch halitosis", especially when forced to work in the close confines of office cubicles. So, unless your goal is to spend the remainder of the day in solitary confinement, skip the pungent, spicy entrees for lunch.

It's even more important for business professionals like financial planners, realtors, dentists and hair dressers to stick to this policy. They can't afford to offend their highly-prized, laboriously-courted clients with clouds of overpowering garlic breath.

And what about the toll this aromatic herb wreaks on romantic encounters? You take your date out to a nice restaurant for dinner, scan the menu and go into breath-paranoia attack. Even the bread sticks are coated with garlic. What's a socially conscious person to do when under siege by popular food trends?

Don't get me wrong. Garlic isn't all bad. There are quite a few tasty dishes that just wouldn't be the same without it. But I'd like to make one small request of the food manufacturers and restaurant chefs who fall into the "garlic abuse" category. Lighten up! Take it easy on the garlic, for heaven's sake. Is this pungent, bulbous herb the only flavor in your recipe arsenal? Could you at least try one dish without it? How about tapping into your creativity and trying basil instead, or thyme, or rosemary?

It's time to take a stand against excessive garlic use and its negative social consequences! (We'll discuss the issues of consuming raw onions at a later date.)

What? You like garlic, you say? Well, go ahead then. Eat that plate of roasted garlic. But you'd better be prepared to cuddle up with a good book because not even your dog will want to get within ten feet of you.

I say, "Bring back the good old days—a time when bad breath was deemed socially unacceptable!"

Does anyone have a breath mint?

A Tangled Web

Parents should be ashamed of themselves for deliberately misleading their kids. If you don't intend to give your child a choice, then why do you tack the question, "Okay?" on to the end of every statement. What's up with that?

When I was a child, my mother would say, "Eat your vegetables, okay?" So when I left the table, she asked, "Where are you going?"

"Out to play," I informed her.

"But you didn't eat your vegetables," she replied.

"Well, you asked me if it was okay, and it's not. I'd rather go play."

"Don't get smart with me," she cried. "Do you want a spanking?"

"Heck no! I just want to go play."

By then, my mother was positively apoplectic; her lips were turning blue. I was six; I had no training in resuscitation techniques.

"Get back to that table and eat your vegetables!" she screeched.

Now that's what I call straightforward communication. Why didn't she just say that in the first place, instead of teasing me with the idea that I actually had a choice in the matter? It's a cruel joke that parents still play on their kids to this very day.

Over time, I came to understand that when my mother asked, "Okay?" what she really meant was, "Do you understand?" I simply became deaf to the "Okay?" part.

Years later, when I was in college, I went to the campus medical clinic because of an upper respiratory infection. In the examination room, the nurse said, "I'm going to give you a shot, okay?"

I braced myself for the sting of the needle, but the nurse paused. "I'm going to give you a shot, okay?" she repeated. I closed my eyes, anticipating the pain, but still she didn't move.

"Do you want the shot or not?" she asked.

"You mean I actually have a choice?" I replied. "You're not just jerking my chain?" I couldn't believe my good fortune. I had finally been elevated to decision-making status. "Cool," I said. "Sure, go ahead."

The nurse paused, reassessing her decision, "Perhaps I should call your mother."

I was positively apoplectic; my lips were turning blue. She recanted and gave me the shot.

The moral of this story, for all you parents out there is this: if you don't intend to give your kid a choice; then don't ask, "Okay?"

Okay?

Overload

For most of us, an automobile is an indispensible part of our lives. We spend tens of thousands of dollars purchasing them and hundreds more to maintain them. We've even added special rooms, called garages, onto our homes just to house and protect our vehicles.

But take a drive through any town in America and you'll find that most of those garages are filled with an over-flow of stuff we don't use or even need, while the expensive car sits outside, exposed to the elements, vandalism or theft. What's up with that?

After my husband, Bob, and I were married, I moved into a house he already owned. He'd been living there for six years and true to American form, his garage was packed front-to-back and side-to-side with stuff—most of which was still in the original moving boxes that arrived when he bought the house.

It seems that the world is divided into two groups—those who can't stand clutter and throw everything out and those who feel the need to hang on to everything they've ever owned. I'm firmly planted in the first category, while my husband hails from the second.

His justification for hoarding, which he learned from his mother, is that he might need each and every one of these items "someday". I acquired my clutter-free tendencies from my mother, whose mantra was, "If you haven't used it in a year, it's taking up valuable space—get rid of it."

I'll have to admit, there have been a few times when I tossed out an item that I needed later on, but never anything that couldn't be purchased again. On the other hand, my husband often needs to buy duplicate items because he just can't find the original underneath that pile of clutter. It's six-in-one/half-a-dozen in the other; the result is about the same with either approach.

But, when I moved into his home, I laid claim to half the garage—my shiny new red coupe was not going to sit outside under the broiling Texas sun.

Bob reluctantly agreed to "clean out the garage", so he and his hoarding mentor, a.k.a. Mom, set aside one weekend to accomplish this monumental, emotionally-wrenching task. Since they both feared my "use-it-or-toss-it" tendencies, I wasn't allowed to participate.

I watched in amazement as they dragged everything from the garage, opened all the boxes, and took an extended trip down "memory lane", examining each treasure. Then they dusted it all off, sorted it into even more boxes and put them back into Bob's designated half of the garage. Apparently I misunderstood; he meant "clean off"—not "clean out".

The contents were now stacked side-to-side, front-to-back and floor-to-ceiling! But he and his mother were positively glowing with pride at their accomplishment.

That evening, I actually managed to pull my car into the garage and had just enough room to squeeze out and slide along the wall of teetering boxes to get to the back door. I made a mental note to beef up my exercise routine. If I gained a single ounce, I wouldn't be able to fit through the opening.

To this very day, I still believe he booby trapped those stacks to come tumbling down with only the slightest bit of motion, just to keep me from sneaking a few boxes out to the trash. It worked—I still have nightmares about being crushed underneath a cardboard avalanche!

Fortunately, that never happened. I did, however, take a wrong turn one evening at the stack marked "Tools" and wound up lost in the "Christmas Decorations" pile. Half an hour later, I finally found the back door.

"Where have you been?" Bob asked.

"Lost in the cardboard jungle," I replied.

Say What?

My dentist is knowledgeable, caring and friendly, and his hygienist does a super job of cleaning my teeth. But, as soon as I'm in the chair with my mouth filled with dental tools and sometimes stuffed with gauze, they expect me to carry on a cheery conversation when the most I can manage is a garbled groan. What's up with that?

I suspect this is a game that all dentists play with their unwitting patients and then share their funniest stories at the annual dental convention.

But I turned the tables on my dentist one day during a routine tooth-filling session. As he injected the analgesic to numb my upper gums, I began to feel my entire body relax as if I'd been anesthetized. "How wonderful," I thought, "I didn't realize modern-day dentistry involved putting patients to sleep to curb their discomfort." Apparently I was mistaken.

He kept up his usual chatter while working diligently on my filling. I could hear him talking, but couldn't respond—I had entered the "Twilight Zone".

When he noticed that I wasn't uttering the standard garbled noises, his tone seemed a bit concerned. He finished his work and announced, "Okay, we're done!"

I tried to sit up, but crashed back down onto the chair. My arm fell off the arm rest and dangled onto the floor.

At first, he thought I had fainted. "Are you feeling light-headed?" he asked.

"No," I mumbled, "Sleepy."

His eyebrows shot up to the top of his head. He glanced at his assistant in horror. "Get the blood pressure cuff!"

They took my pulse, measured my blood pressure, rubbed my hands briskly and, thankfully, didn't resort to slapping my face to encourage me to wake up. After determining that I was not in medical distress and conferring secretly in their corner, they decided to let me sleep it off in the dental chair under their watchful gaze.

I felt somewhat guilty holding one of their chairs hostage, given the fact that it probably generated roughly $2,000 per hour in revenue, but my arms and legs felt like rubber; I couldn't move. And where else could they put me? It might be a tad awkward to explain to other patients why there was a woman lying on the floor. Talk about a lively conversation!

When I finally managed to stagger out to the waiting room, Susan, the receptionist, stopped me at the door. "The doctor wants you to wait here for awhile just to make sure you've recovered."

"But I'm starving," I replied. "I'll just walk next door and get a sandwich."

She frowned and put her hands on her hips to protest.

"I'm going to faint if I don't get some food soon!" I argued.

She flinched at the thought of dealing with another motionless body episode and recanted. "Bring it back here," she admonished. "You need to stay a bit longer before you drive home."

Ten minutes later I was settled into a chair in the waiting room, scarfing down my tasty turkey sandwich. As other patients filed in, they eyed my unusual dental-office protocol, clearly coveting my food.

"Are they serving lunch at the dentist's office these days?" one matronly woman snipped.

"Only if you survive the procedure," I replied.

Her eyes widened with fear and she grabbed the arms of her chair in a white-knuckled grip.

"Ahem!" Susan growled at me. "I think it's safe for you to leave now," she oogled, snapping her head toward the door.

I smiled innocently, crumpled my sandwich wrapper and stuffed it in my pocket. Then I stood, waivered slightly for effect and headed for the exit.

"Everything will be just fine, Mrs. Logan," Susan cooed, while prying the woman's fingers off the chair. She nudged the reluctant patient toward the dentist waiting in the back.

"I'll have t-t-tuna," the woman stuttered, "on wh-wheat."

I'm sure my dentist will be sharing my story at the annual dentist's convention. It won't, however, be in the "funniest patient story" category, but the scariest.

I now have the words "BIZARRE" written in big red letters across the top of my medical chart. And I'm quite certain it refers to more than just my unusual reaction to the medication. The receptionist underlined the word with her shocking pink highlighter pen—TWICE!

The Sign
Spoke to Me!

Four-letter words have long been known for getting us into trouble—first with our parents and teachers; then later on, with society. But there's one socially acceptable four-letter word that can wreak havoc on our lives in general and our budgets in particular. We encounter it at every turn and its hypnotic appeal pulls us in like a magnet—"SALE!"

This word has the same affect on all of us: young and old, male and female, we simply cannot escape its allure; the greater the discount—the bigger the temptation. It doesn't matter whether we need the item or can even afford the item, we can't resist a sale! What's up with that?

We're bombarded with sale announcements on a daily basis: through the mail, on the radio, on television, and with huge signs plastered in store windows. How can we avoid the onslaught? Grocery stores, furniture stores, sporting goods stores, department stores, even the Internet—they're all lying in wait, ready to cast their "discount spells" to relieve us of our hard-earned cash.

The super warehouse stores are some of the worst offenders. "Ten pounds of bacon for ten dollars!" Wow! Never mind that you can't eat it all before it spoils, or if you did you'd be one hundred pounds overweight and probably drop dead of a heart attack. But, hey! You saved twenty dollars on bacon!

My husband and I went shopping for new stainless steel eating utensils. We found a pattern we liked in a set of twelve and discovered it was on sale for seventy-five percent off.

"Let's get two sets," was my husband's immediate response.

"Why do we need twenty-four forks?" I asked. "I don't have enough space to store that many."

"But we're saving a hundred dollars!" he exclaimed.

Women are particularly vulnerable when they find shoes on sale. "Buy five pair and get two pair free!" Never mind that you only need one pair. If you spend five times more than you intended and buy five times more than you need, you'll get two pair free.

Even if you do your bargain hunting at garage sales, the spending can add up in a hurry. Haggling is addictive. It's quite a power-rush to talk the owner down from two dollars to one dollar on your twenty-third pair of blue-bird salt-and-pepper shakers. What a coup!

These days you don't even need to leave the comfort of your home to indulge your "sales habit". Just download your cash to anywhere in the world with the click of a button on the computer.

If we all continue to succumb to the overwhelming power of "The Sale", we'll save ourselves right into bankruptcy. This scenario might play out as follows:

"So, how did you wind up in this terrible predicament?" the bankruptcy judge will ask.

"It was on sale!" you'll reply. "I already had four push lawn mowers, but this was a riding lawn mower, with a 26 horsepower V-twin engine and a fifty-four inch deck. It was half off!"

"Wow!" the judge exclaims. "Is it still on sale? I need one of those."

"Sure," your lawyer confirms. "I got three for myself."

So, how does the average, hard-working American resist the power of "The Sale?"

Don't ask me! The half-price book store is my home away from home; my best friend is a garage-sale junkie; and my eighty-year-old mother has three closets jammed with brand new clothes, which she got on sale, of course.

I guess you'll realize that you need help when you're living off peanut butter sandwiches and raiding your kid's piggy bank to buy gas for your car.

Until then...Happy Shopping!

Stuffed!

What could be more comforting than Thanksgiving dinner shared with extended family members? (Okay, hold the snickering—I mean, aside from the occasional personality clashes and unavoidable family tiffs.)

We gather together on this traditional holiday to express our thanks for the bounty we have received throughout the year. And judging by the mountain of food piled on the table, which literally groans under the sheer weight of it all—for most of us it's a sign of more than plenty.

But the scariest part about this holiday is the fact that the weight of that food is about to be transferred from the table to everyone surrounding it. After all, Thanksgiving spelled backwards is "gluttony"—at least metaphorically speaking. But it doesn't matter whether you spell it upside down, inside out or backwards, the bottom line is that on this "holy day of food worshipping", it seems that we grant ourselves a free pass to scarf down everything in sight. What's up with that?

Statistics show that the average person consumes roughly 6,000 calories on Thanksgiving Day—nearly three times the amount we eat on any regular day. What causes us to turn into human vacuum cleaners this one day of the year? I suspect that it involves the same reasoning as the famous "mountain climbing" quote.

"Why did you climb Mount Everest?"

"Because it was there."

"Why did you eat five pounds of turkey, a dozen dinner rolls and two pumpkin pies?"

"Because they were there."

We simply have no willpower when tasty homemade food is placed within our grasp. Then we spend the rest of the day in a comatose state sitting in front of the television.

I guess it really doesn't matter, since there's absolutely no way we could burn off that many calories. It would take 12 hours of non-stop jogging or 24 hours of walking. And that is SO not going to happen. You can just stuff that exercise nonsense right up the turkey where it belongs! This is a holiday!

Year after year we indulge ourselves in at least one serving of each and every one of the twenty-eight or more offerings from the Thanksgiving Day spread, and then, when we're about to explode, the hostess offers dessert.

"Do you want pecan pie, apple pie, or pumpkin pie?" she asks.

"Sure," we reply. Why pick just one when we can have all three?

I guess we'll never know why we lose all sense of reason on this special day. I believe it must have its roots somewhere in our early evolution, tied to Cro-Magnon Man's fear of famine—or we just plain have no will power when our senses are overloaded with so much taste-tempting, mouth-watering, aromatic, delectable treats. Yep, that's probably it.

And we're darn thankful to have them, too. Bring on the turkey! Could you pass the sweet potatoes again, please?

Visions of Sugar Plums

When I was seven, my mother arranged for my two sisters, ages five and nine, and me to take ballet classes at our local community center. We purchased the requisite black leotards, pink tights and ballet slippers, which I laid out carefully beside my bed. I could barely contain my anticipation for the first day of class.

We donned our ballet attire and were chauffeured to the community center at the appointed time. I was in ballerina heaven and practiced every move with serious determination. Visions of Sugar Plum Fairies danced in my head.

When my mother collected us an hour later, I was flushed with excitement and couldn't wait for the next class. My two sisters, however, wanted no part of the ballet life and refused to go back. Apparently, the activity decisions in our family were decided by democratic vote, so my ballet career began and ended in one day. It was the first time I ever said, "What's up with that? Life just isn't fair!"

Many years later, when I was in my mid-thirties, I noticed an ad in our neighborhood newsletter for an adult ballet exercise class. I couldn't get to the phone fast enough to sign up. The visions of Sugar Plum Fairies had returned and this time, no one could stand in my way. Once again, I purchased the required black leotard, pink tights and ballet slippers—ballerina heaven, here I come.

There were eight of us middle-aged to older-aged women in the class—apparently all deprived of our childhood dreams to be prima ballerinas; ethereal visions in tulle. We pirouetted, pliéd and chasséd our hearts out, up and down the wooden floor in the mirrored studio. But, alas, there would be no Nutcracker Suite performances for us.

It turned out to be a wonderful exercise class, but my fantasy of wearing a beautiful tulle costume and dancing in the spotlight with the Nutcracker Prince would never come to pass. Or at least that's what I thought, until one day, many years later when I was in my mid-fifties, and an invitation to the First Annual Neighborhood Costume Party arrived in the mail.

My ballerina dream bubbled to the surface, and I made a beeline to the fabric store to purchase yards and yards of pink tulle. For days, I worked on my costume. Then one afternoon, I pranced into the living room and twirled around for my husband, Bob, to admire. I was a slightly plump, gray-haired vision in tulle.

He pushed the mute button on the television to silence the sirens blaring from his favorite police reality show. "Very nice," he smiled.

"I'm the Sugar Plum Fairy," I explained. "And you will be my Nutcracker Prince," I added, holding up a man's formal red jacket, complete with tails, and a spectacular hat with a fluffy plume."

"Hmm," was his suspicious reply. "Where are the pants?"

Dang, I was busted! Reluctantly, I held up a pair of men's white tights.

He raised one eyebrow and pressed the mute button again. The sirens blared from the television speakers as the good guys continued their pursuit of the bad guys.

I knew it was a long shot, but I had to try.

On the night of the big event, I finally realized my Sugar Plum Fairy dream; it had taken me nearly fifty years. I wasn't dancing around a stage on pointed ballerina shoes, but my ballet slippers were tied with pink satin ribbons, my tulle skirt swirled around me like a cloud, and my rhinestone tiara sparkled under the dance floor spotlights.

Bob chose to wear a gangster costume, with a black pinstripe suit, black shirt and tie and a fedora hat. But his favorite accessory was the fake Tommy gun that he slung jauntily over his shoulder. He was the infamous mobster, Nicky "The Nutcracker" Scarpetti.

He wasn't quite the "Nutcracker Prince" that I had envisioned, but a prince by any other name is still a prince!

It was a magical evening.

Share Your "What's Up With That?" Ideas

I love to receive feedback from my readers and would especially like to hear your "what's up with that?" tales.

If you'd like to share your own frustrating dilemmas from everyday life, e-mail your comments to:

gloria@bluesagepress.com

Or send them in writing to:

Gloria Lyons
Blue Sage Press
48 Borondo Pines
La Marque, TX 77568

Just remember to keep it light and keep it tactful, because life is semi-humorous.

About the Author

Gloria Hander Lyons has channeled 30 years of training and hands-on experience in the areas of art, interior decorating, crafting and event planning into writing creative how-to books. Her books cover a wide range of topics including decorating your home, cooking, planning weddings and tea parties, crafting and self-publishing, plus humorous slice-of-life short stories.

Gloria has designed original craft projects featured in magazines, such as *Better Homes and Gardens, McCall's, Country Handcrafts* and *Crafts*. She teaches interior decorating and self-publishing classes at her local community college.

Visit her website for free craft ideas, decorating and event planning tips and tasty recipes: www.BlueSagePress.com.

Send questions or comments to:

gloria@bluesagepress.com

Ordering Information

To order additional copies of this book, send check or money order payable to Gloria Lyons to: Blue Sage Press, 48 Borondo Pines, La Marque, TX 77568.

Cost for this edition is $6.95 per book (U.S. currency only) plus $3.00 shipping and handling for the first book and $1.50 for each additional book shipped to the same U.S. address. Texas residents add 8.25% sales tax to total order amount.

To pay by credit card or get a complete list of books written by Gloria Hander Lyons, visit our website at:

www.BlueSagePress.com

Other Books by Gloria Hander Lyons

- Easy Microwave Desserts in a Mug
- Easy Microwave Desserts in a Mug for Kids
- No Rules – Just Fun Decorating
- Just Fun Decorating for Tweens & Teens
- Decorating Basics: For Men Only
- Ten Common Home Decorating Mistakes & How to Avoid Them
- If Teapots Could Talk—Fun Ideas for Tea Parties
- The Super-Bride's Guide for Dodging Wedding Pitfalls
- Lavender Sensations: Fragrant Herbs for Home & Bath
- A Taste of Lavender: Delectable Treats with an Exotic Floral Flavor
- Designs That Sell: How to Make Your Home Show Better & Sell Faster
- Self-Publishing on a Budget: A Do-It-All-Yourself Guide
- The Secret Ingredient: Tasty Recipes with an Unusual Twist
- Hand Over the Chocolate & No One Gets Hurt: The Chocolate-Lover's Cookbook
- Flamingos, Poodle Skirts & Red Hots: Creative Theme Party Ideas
- Quick Gifts From the Kitchen: No Cooking Required
- 40 Favorite Impossible Pies: Main Dishes & Desserts
- A Taste of Memories: Comforting Foods From Our Past
- Pearls of Wisdom for Creating a Joyful Life

For a complete list of books written by Gloria Hander Lyons, visit our website at:

www.BlueSagePress.com

www.ingramcontent.com/pod-product-compliance
Lightning Source LLC
Chambersburg PA
CBHW060610030426
42337CB00018B/3024